PRAISE FOR

N o t e s o n
C O O K I N G

"In *Notes on Cooking*, Lauren Braun Costello and Russell Reich bring you indispensable advice, experience, and know-how of many great chefs. This handsome book is both inspirational and practical, and a superb addition to the library of any passionate cook."

— Daniel Boulud, Chef, Restaurant Daniel

"Concise, focused, and sensible. *Notes on Cooking* is full of useful advice for young chefs. Well worth reading."

— Jacques Pépin, Chef, Cookbook Author,
and PBS–TV Cooking Series Host

"*Notes on Cooking* is exactly what it says it is: a short guide to an essential craft. There's enough wisdom here to inspire any home cook or seasoned professional."

— Dan Barber, Executive Chef/Co–Owner, Blue Hill

"I wish *Notes on Cooking* had been written about 35 years ago, when I started cooking professionally. It is an excellent source of level-headed, practical, and essential advice; an indispensable and wonderfully succinct compendium of knowledge for anyone, both veteran and novice, who is involved with food preparation."

— Michael Romano, Chef,
Union Square Hospitality Group

Notes on
COOKING

Notes on
COOKING

*A Short Guide
to an Essential Craft*

LAUREN BRAUN
COSTELLO

RUSSELL
REICH

Notes on Cooking: A Short Guide to an Essential Craft
by Lauren Braun Costello and Russell Reich

© 2009 by RCR Creative Press Incorporated. Printed and bound in the United States of America. All rights reserved. First printing 2009.

Published by RCR Creative Press Incorporated, New York, New York

Jacket design by Julia Reich and Daniel Tamman. Illustrations by Eric Kittelberger and Daniel Tamman. Interior design by Pneuma Books, LLC.

Also by Russell Reich
Notes on Directing: 130 Lessons in Leadership from the Director's Chair

Also by Lauren Braun Costello
The Competent Cook: Essential Tools, Techniques, and Recipes for the Modern At—Home Cook

Cataloging–in–Publication
(Provided by The Donohue Group)

Costello, Lauren Braun.
  Notes on cooking : a short guide to an essential craft / Lauren Braun Costello, Russell Reich ; [afterword by Dorothy Hamilton].

  p. : ill. ; cm. -- (Notes on--)

  Includes bibliographical references and index.
  ISBN: 978-0-9724255-1-3

1. Cookery--Handbooks, manuals, etc. 2. Cookery--Quotations, maxims, etc.
I. Reich, Russell, 1963- II. Hamilton, Dorothy M. III. Title.

TX652 .C67 2009
641.5   2008939351

PRINTED AND BOUND IN THE UNITED STATES OF AMERICA
on acid∞free paper

18 17 16 15 14 13 12 11 10 09   01 02 03 04 05 06 07 08 09 10

RcR CREATIVE PRESS

NEW YORK

DEDICATED TO
MARCIA S. COHEN

AND IN MEMORY OF
FRANK HAUSER

Table of Contents

Table of Contents

Table of Contents

Table of Contents

Table of Contents

Notes on
Notes on Cooking

by Lauren Braun Costello

A recipe is like a road map. A road map shows you where to go and how to get there, but does not teach you how to drive. A recipe lists ingredients and quantities and what you need to do with them, but does not teach you how to cook. It is merely procedural and does not tell you how to select your ingredients, how to recognize quality, why to simmer instead of boil, when to adjust the heat, how to develop flavor, how to season a dish... or any of a hundred other considerations that compose how to *think* like a cook.

While training under and later working with great chefs, I learned undisputed cooking truths applicable across time and culture that are seldom learned outside a professional setting—and rarely from a recipe book. Yet the cooking standards based on these long–held but not widely shared absolutes can help anyone become a better cook.

Now I carry the lessons and standards of my teachers into every kitchen in which I cook. Chef Henri Viain reminds me always to "flag" a hot pan. Chef Sixto Alonso insists that no good sauce is made from water. My mentor, Chef Michel Nischan, impresses on me the highest standard for straining a stock: "Bone dry," he keeps saying. "Bone dry." And Master Chef André Soltner teaches me that simple presentation — where the cook's hand is invisible — is a sign of refinement. These timeless culinary truths, codes of conduct, and simple gems of wisdom are as important to me as any procedure, implement, or ingredient.

I alone am responsible for the soul and standards that I bring to the table. But I falter. As a student in his class, I once burned Chef Henri by failing to flag a hot pan. I have made sauce with water when I neglected first to check that I had enough chicken stock on hand. How did I learn that lesson about straining stock? The hard way, by leaving the last drop of stock on the wrong side of the *chinois*. And, oh, have I overgarnished!

I confess my sins. Yet the standards remain. The lesson? The unfailing commitment of any serious cook is not to perfection, but to the *idea* of perfection, to excellence.

With a deep desire to share this idea and to capture what I have come to understand to be true, to be of the highest standard, and of unchanging value, I wondered: How can I best communicate such sensibilities effectively?

Russell Reich, a participant in one of my cooking series, had the answer. One day after class, he approached me with a copy of his previous book, *Notes on Directing*, and asked what I thought I could do with the topic of cooking using the "Notes" format. He explained the virtue of the approach: A note dares shamelessly to assert The Truth. It is not weighed down by prevarications or extraneous information; the fat is cut away and only the essence remains. "All gold, no rocks" is how one critic described it. I recognized immediately how the lessons I had learned and sought to teach could be expressed succinctly and boldly.

When we began, I supplied the expertise from the cooking world, and Russell, director and writer that he is, provided both the sensibility of the book's voice and the perspective of the reader. Students often have useful insights, however, and cooks can be pretty good at expressing themselves in all sorts of ways. That is how our collaboration evolved, and over time our roles became shared, even blurred. One might say the content of the book is an emulsion of the ingredients we each provided.

We also intend *Notes on Cooking* to be a reduction. What remains is a concentration of the culinary craft. Adopt these prescriptions as your own, or defy them with conviction and purpose. Either way, you then will be meaningfully committed to the craft and will undoubtedly establish a few new standards of your own.

OCTOBER 2008

xxiii

More Notes on
Notes on Cooking

In addition to being of interest to the aspiring cook, this book will serve as a helpful stimulant to the experienced practitioner open to considering new perspectives or ways of working. It is also for the gourmand, epicure, gourmet, or gastronome who wishes to peer more closely into the hidden, alchemical process of cooking.

This book aims to be short, as well as immediately useful or insightful. In general, it is an account of how to think and work like a cook, and it is meant to save time — the cook's and everyone else's. Used as a tool, it can be read in at least three directions:

1. A linear approach from start to finish tracks roughly through the cooking process, addressing the cook's concerns in the general order they are likely to arise.

2. A random, pointillist approach is also appropriate. For instance, while on the way to the grocer or waiting for the dough to rise, open the book to wherever whimsy dictates and get a taste of just what might be needed for that day's preparations.

3. A crisscross line of attack emerges by following the occasional cross—references from note to note. These connections reveal conceptual relationships and highlight larger themes that might not be readily apparent across relatively broad expanses of the material.

There are no recipes here; those are easily found elsewhere in abundant quantity and high quality. In their place are the timeless and essential clarifications, distillations, reductions, concentrations, and extractions of cooking wisdom that great culinary experts have learned and practiced and passed on for decades, even centuries.

We have given the book the voice of an assertive but encouraging instructor, one whose favorite words are "do this," "don't do that," "always," and "never." We could have taken a milder, more suggestive approach, but better, we thought, to overshoot and provoke than to risk having all the impact of a marshmallow.

More Notes on Notes on Cooking

Certainly it is appropriate to question the dogmatic assertions found here, to test them, debate them, hate them even. Our hope, though, is that the reader will have nearly an impossible time *ignoring* them.

The reader, for example, will likely find contradictions within these pages (such as the conflicting directives to follow the recipe and to depart from it). But just as any cook must choose his or her tools and tactics every moment of each meal or service, the reader will have to discern when to apply a particular truth and when to be alert to its exceptions and contradictions.

Like most things in life, cooking must be learned and understood not through words, but through practice. You must continually taste, touch, smell, look at, and listen to the food; your own senses and sensibilities will teach you more than will any book. The inevitable failures, delightful discoveries, and unanticipated rewards that arise from persistence, experimentation, commitment, and repetition are for you as a cook to earn on your own.

We are what we repeatedly do.
Excellence, then, is not an act,
but a habit.

ARISTOTLE (384 BC — 322 BC)

I

*Understanding
the Recipe*

1. Read the recipe.

Turn off the television, don't answer the phone, just sit and read it through. Make a mental inventory of the sort of equipment you need, the cooking techniques required, the ingredients you have on hand. Note the stages of preparation, and get a sense of appropriate timings.

2. Read it again.

This time let your mind wander. Think about the finished look of the dish, the aromas, the flavors, the textures you want to create, and whether any questions you had the first time around are answering themselves.

3. Read at least three similar recipes.

Making *boeuf bourguignon*? Before you begin, study at least three ways to do it. Take, for instance, Craig Claiborne's use of wine *and* cognac, Julia Child's delayed use of aromatics (added halfway through the cooking process), and Richard Olney's guidance on the right cut of meat (a gelatinous cut such as oxtail, shank, heel, or chuck).

4. If it's in the title, leave it alone.

Don't mess with core ingredients. Good recipes are designed around particular flavors. If you are considering a recipe of *boeuf bourguignon* and don't care for beef or Burgundy wine, find a different recipe.

5. Target the result more than the timing.

The time noted might not be accurate. Consider the unfortunate possibility that the writer might not have tested the recipe, but the desired result is certain. If the recipe says "stir onions for 20 minutes until softened and browned," and after 15 minutes the onions are soft and brown, stop.

Note the time it takes *you* with *your* equipment and record that change for the next time you prepare the dish.

6. Recognize that recipes are often compromises.

Editors, considering the collective palate of the publication's audience, sometimes urge recipe writers to tone things down for wider appeal. The quantities indicated might not reflect your, or even the writer's, true preference.

If you sense from a lifetime of eating and cooking that two teaspoons of a spice or an herb will not do, add more.

7. **When you're ready, mess with the recipe.**

   "Life," writes Ray Bradbury, "is trying things to see if they work."

8. **Do it again.**

   Repetition of the recipe is the path to refinement. You'll learn something every time.

9. **Do not be surprised by surprising results.**

   You can never control it all. The humidity in the room, the quality of your water, the nature of your fire, the chemistry of your cookware—all sorts of variables are at play. There might be no way to know them all, but do expect uncertainties.

10. **Your soul is in the food.**

    Twenty–four cooks assigned to the same mayonnaise recipe—the same bowls, same spoons, same eggs, same mustard, same oil, same whisks, same peppermills, same measuring cups, same room, same time of day, same marching orders—will create twenty–four different mayonnaises.

Here's why: *All* of the cook's sensibilities and emotions make a difference. Strength, speed, rhythm, even delicacy or aggression translate to the dish. You get different chemical results based on what you bring to the table.

II

---◆⟨≋⟩◆---

The Cook's Role

11. **The cook's first job is to delight.**
    Your first identity is as sensualist, then nutritionist, captain, aesthete, or anything else. Lure with aroma, entice with color, disarm with texture, seduce with flavor.

12. **Feed others as they wish to be fed.**
    The Golden Rule: Prepare the dish as you would want to enjoy it yourself.
    The Platinum Rule: Prepare the dish as the person eating it wishes it to be.

13. **Feed others as only you can feed them.**
    Yes, you want to please them, but know, too, they want *you* to do it. That means bringing your substantial and unique contributions into the mix.

14. Work from your strength.

Don't try to master everything. Become known for a few dishes, perhaps even the near perfection of one. Discover your obsession, then make yourself a slave to it: the mastery of a traditional dish, the combination of ingredients that have never before met, precision in presentation, devotion to a culinary heritage, the introduction of color where it never before existed...

15. Aim at mastery of craft, not at art.

Know the basics. Repeat and practice, and the sublime will rise at rare, unexpected moments. Be open to capturing art when it comes, but craft is your highest daily priority.

16. Don't TRY to be different.

You are different. Cook from your gut.

17. Embrace the mundane.

Do not bemoan the pedestrian tasks. Find pleasure in peeling a carrot, steaming rice, searing a steak, prepping, cleaning. Your reward is *in* the work, not around it.

Cooking is not about convenience, but the pleasure earned through creation and in giving pleasure to others. Shortcuts are tempting, even necessary from time to time.

But if you rely on pre—cut vegetables, pre—marinated meats, and canned sauces, you are not cooking. You are assembling.

18. **Cook globally.**

Apply the thematic greatness of diverse cuisines to your cooking. The French taught us to build flavor with aromatics, stocks, and sauces. The Chinese gifted us with the pass—through process of locking in flavor with hot oil or water before stir—frying. Enhance your cooking using such techniques and sensibilities.

In Indian cooking, spices often are toasted before being ground. (To toast in this case means heating at low to medium heat in a dry pan until your nose tells you it is ready.) Toasting deepens and darkens both flavor and aroma, like turning up the volume on everything the spices offer. This is genius. Toasted coriander, for instance, smells like popcorn and oranges.

19. **Justify your food in at least two ways.**

A dish must taste good *and* be seasonal, or look good *and* be healthful. Having dual objectives raises your standard of execution. Plus, when a single purpose falls short, you have provided yourself a safety net.

20. **Please, PLEASE slow down.**

    To save time, avoid injuries, and do better work, don't rush. No frantic action. First, master your craft, then *earn* speed as the external expression of internal fluency.

21. **Above all, do no harm.**

    Primum non nocere. As both Curnonsky, the "Prince of Gastronomy," and the great Alice Waters admonish: let things taste of what they are. Know the product and let it be.

22. **Dare to do less.**

    Do not pull every trick from your toque when you cook. There is a time and a place for every technique, flavor combination, ingredient, and plating style. You will get the chance. For now, do merely what the food requires.

    "Simplicity," writes Leonardo da Vinci, "is the ultimate sophistication." (See 209. True refinement is invisible.)

23. **Preside happily over accidents.**

    Get in the habit of celebrating errors and seeking lessons. The unrisen soufflé, the broken sauce, the tough sirloin, the curdled *crème anglaise*—every mistake is a chance to turn misfortune to education and, in some cases, discovery.

    A famous example: In 1889, Stéphanie Tatin left her apples cooking in butter and sugar for too long and risked drying or even burning them. She rescued the dish by covering the apples with pastry to protect them as they finished in the oven, then turning the dish upside down, with its apple base now on *top*. The result became a classic: *tarte Tatin*, upside–down apple tart.

24. Don't be grim.

Meal preparation should be demanding and enjoyable. So should you.

25. The best compliment for a cook...

"More, please." Or speechlessness. Or, in some cultures, a belch.

26. Eat.

Just as a good writer must read, a good cook must eat. Know the experience of receiving and consuming food at least as well as you know the experience of preparing and serving it.

III

Tools & Equipment

27. Nothing about a kitchen should be dark.

The presence of heat and sharp objects argues against it, as does the need for spotlessness. Also, light is appropriate to the place that signifies life, energy, and sustenance.

28. Cook for the kitchen you're in.

Consider the reality of your workspace. Identify and accept its benefits and constraints. If your kitchen has no windows or ventilation, broil the chicken instead of grilling it on the stovetop. Do not attempt to roast a 20—pound turkey in a kitchenette's half oven. If you only have counter space for the cutting board but not for rolling dough, make apple pie, not apple strudel.

29. Obtain the basics.

It is less expensive and more productive in the long run to buy one quality knife than multiple inferior ones. This is

13

true for most other equipment as well. For a brief, anno-tated inventory of essentials, see appendix 3.

30. **Care for your knives.**

Sharpen your knives up to several times a week so you never have a "rolled," or dull, edge. Use a whetstone to raise a burr, and hone with a sharpening steel as needed to refresh the blade. Clean and dry thoroughly after each sharpening. If you are a professional cook, you are already doing all this, of course. If you're a home cook, consult a cutlery pro.

To ensure longevity, use wood or plastic cutting boards. Marble, glass, and ceramic will dull or chip the blade, pro-vide no "bite" for the blade, and encourage slippage.

Never scrape the sharp edge across the cutting board. To gather food bits — either waste or choppings — turn your knife over and scrape with the spine of the blade.

Never put a knife in the dishwasher. Hot water dulls the blade. Wash your knives in warm, soapy water and dry them immediately with a clean towel.

Never leave knives soaking in the sink. This is bad for the blade and dangerous should you reach in, unaware.

Never use your knife for anything other than breaking down foods; it is not a can opener, box cutter, or screw-driver.

31. **Hold the knife's handle and blade properly.**

    A very important note: three fingers around the handle; thumb and forefinger *pinching the blade*. No other technique provides greater control or safety.

32. **Dress for the job.**

    In an environment of things hot, heavy, and sharp, covered limbs and feet are compulsory. Long sleeves. Hair pulled back and covered. Rings off. Professionals do not wear those double–breasted white jackets merely to resemble members of a brigade; protection from burns and cuts is essential.

33. **Carry two towels.**

    One for each hand. Not primarily to wipe smudges and spills, but to pick up hot things safely. (See also 93. Don't grab a hot pan with a wet cloth.)

34. **Do not wear perfume or cologne while you cook.**

    Anything that inhibits or distracts your senses is inappropriate in a kitchen. Banish fragranced candles, counter sprays, soaps, and lotions. Let only your ingredients and their chemical transformation scent the air.

35. **Banter down.**

    In a professional setting, there should be no voices louder

than the symphony of banging pots, boiling water, sizzling, and chopping. Don't stop chopping, stop *talking*. Focus on your task. You need all your senses at the ready, without distraction.

36. Use your hands and fingers.
Julia Child was fond of saying that a cook's best tool is her hands. As long as those parts are clean, pick up, grab on, dig in. Connect directly to your ingredients.

37. Never use your hands and fingers to taste.
A cook never moves from hand to mouth. A clean fork or spoon does the job just as well. Good manners require it. Sanitation demands it.

38. Be wary of single—use gadgets.
A skilled cook with a chef's knife, for example, can make better garlic paste — with no waste — than any garlic press ever could. An avocado slicer? Onion dicer? Herb stripper? No.

39. Use wet measures for liquids, dry measures for solids.
Yes, there is a difference, negligible in small—scale recipes, but significant when larger volumes apply. A reliable indicator of which is which: wet measuring cups tend to have spouts, dry cups do not.

IV

❈

Procurement & Storage

40. **Use what you have.**

    A good cook wastes nothing. Before you run to the store to buy new ingredients, make use of what is already in your kitchen.

41. **Shop locally.**

    Support your local farmers and artisanal producers who take pride in their products and are less likely to use pesticides, preservatives, or hormones. Sustain your regional culinary heritage and its indigenous crops. Tie yourself to the land and its seasons. Connect yourself to the cycle of nature.

    Too abstract? Then consider this functional benefit: If you are prone to seasonal allergies, buy and eat local honey. Local bees collect pollen from local flora. Eating continual small doses of their honey can act like a series of immunology injections, strengthening your tolerance and lessening your allergic discomfort.

Aside from the cultural and medical benefits of local ingredients, there are culinary advantages, including speed to market and inherent freshness. "Shipping is a terrible thing to do to vegetables," writes Elizabeth Berry. "They probably get jet–lagged, just like people."

42. Learn from your farmer.

Chef Michel Nischan says, "One of the things I've learned in the role of chef–as–student: The farmer is often your teacher." The farmer plays midwife to the ingredient, knows it best, and often can tell you how to cook it properly.

43. Hand–select your ingredients.

Shopping for groceries by telephone or online is a convenient and increasingly common practice, but you lose a level of control over the finished product. Don't let someone else do the choosing for you. Only you know what your dishes and sensibilities require.

44. Shop seasonally.

You can procure nearly anything you want whenever you want it. That does not mean you should. Summer strawberries picked ripe from the bush are ruby red, juicy, supple, and sweet — a far cry from their winterized counterparts that are torched with a heat lamp before their time (note their bitter white centers).

Fresh ingredients serve as a vital seasonal clock and humble us to wait until properly enjoyed.

45. A dish is only as good as what goes into it.
Garbage in, garbage out. Buy the best ingredients you can afford. (See 193. If you won't drink it, don't cook with it.)

46. Don't be seduced by a high price.
Expensive items might not be intrinsically good, just out of season and therefore difficult to procure. Hard–to–get is not, in itself, a virtue. Spare yourself the cost of scarcity and enjoy yet another benefit of procuring locally and seasonally.

47. Use fresh ingredients.
The fresher the ingredient, by definition, the more alive it is, a quality that translates immediately to the plate and palate. A freshly caught fish bares the flavor of the water it came from even after it has been cooked. Arugula picked right from the soil boasts a grassy and peppery tone. Freshly made mozzarella manifests its superior, sweet, milky essence by appearance as well as taste.

48. Date and label perishables.

It is more reliable than remembering what you stored when.

49. Rotate your product.

Shelve your perishables with the newest in the back and oldest in the front. Habituate yourself to the FIFO system: First In First Out.

50. Do not use metal for storage.

Metal can leach metallic flavors into food, and acidic food can eat through metals, such as aluminum foil, in as little as a day. Acidic marinades, for example, require a non—reactive container such as glass, ceramic, or plastic.

51. Store non—perishables in a cool, dry place.

Never in direct sunlight. Thank goodness your pantry doesn't have a window.

52. Always store cooked foods above raw foods in the refrigerator.

Never put raw meat on a shelf above the cheesecake. When raw juices drip, bacteria spread.

53. Practice individual quick freezing.

Prevent the formation of giant, gnarled boulders of frozen food. Set each piece of like items with ample space on a sheet pan and place in the freezer. Once the individual food items are frozen, *then* place them together in a plastic bag and back in the freezer. Because they were individually frozen first, they will never form into a solid block.

And surely you know not to freeze raw chicken and broccoli *together*. (See 68. Do not cross—contaminate.)

54. Keep cold foods cold, hot foods hot.

Store cold foods below 40°F (about 5°C) and hold hot foods above 135°F (57°C). In between is the Food Temperature Danger Zone, where bacteria can grow rapidly.

55. Do not defrost on the counter.

Defrosting foods on the countertop puts them in the Food Temperature Danger Zone. Defrost frozen meats and seafood in the refrigerator, in a bowl of cold water, or under cold running water.

56. Do not store frozen foods indefinitely.

Even at typical freezer temperatures, some bacteria are still active. Label all your frozen foods to ensure safety. Sealed properly, meats can be frozen for up to nine months, and fish and vegetables for up to six months, depending on their initial quality.

57. When something smells fishy, it is also likely rotten.
If it doesn't smell right, it isn't. When in doubt, throw it out. Now. (See 144. Fish should not smell.)

58. One week is enough.
After one week in the refrigerator, freshly prepared foods and leftovers should be tossed. Just throw them away.

There are noteworthy exceptions to the one–week rule, including sushi, ceviche, and other raw dishes. Consume or toss those within one day.

V

Mise en place

59. Mise en place. Always.

Literally "put in place," *mise en place* [MEEZ ahn plahs] might just as well mean "take time to save time."

Wash, peel, cut, measure, and select *before* you begin the cooking process. Set out each measured ingredient, ready to play its part. Don't get caught in the rush to start cooking. If you surge ahead, you'll just have to stop and take time to prepare what should have been *mise en place* in the first place — and you'll end up burning the sauce.

60. Mise en place your equipment.

Gather what you need before you begin to cook. Have the tongs ready the moment the chicken needs turning. Determine early, before the critical moment, if they're still in the dishwasher.

61. Your station is your reputation.

You can't build from bad prep. That is why your *mise en place* says more about you and your cooking than anything else aside from your finished food. Your end is in your beginning.

62. Wash your hands.

Warm water: 100°F (38°C). Soap. Thirty seconds of scrubbing, *minimum*, between the fingers, the back of the hands, and under the nails. Use a nailbrush. This is the only way to be truly clean, and a clean cook is essential to safe cooking.

63. Don't touch your face.

Your itchy nose beckons? Resist. Failed to resist? Wash again.

64. Stabilize your work surfaces.

Put a wet paper towel underneath your cutting board to keep it from slipping. This makes knife work safer.

Likewise, shape a rag into a donut and place it beneath your bowl so it does not wobble. When making vinaigrette, for instance, you need one hand to whisk and the other to pour the oil slowly and steadily. The towel holds the bowl while you mix.

Alternatively, buy a board and bowls with rubber bottoms made for precisely this purpose.

65. Peel, PARE, then cut.

You *peel* to rid a fruit or vegetable of its outer skin; you *cut* to achieve the final shape and size desired.

In between, you *pare*, for two reasons: The first is to create a flat surface on which to stabilize a wobbly, curved, and possibly slippery item. The second is to sculpt or form the product in preparation for final cutting. Cubing a potato? First peel the potato, then pare it into a rectangular block, then into rectangular slabs, then into sticks, *then* cut into cubes.

66. Group like tasks.

If you are baking an apple pie, peel ALL the apples first, then chop them. Do not peel and chop each one before moving on to the next. A cook earns speed using this expeditious, efficient, and organized way to work.

67. Clean as you go.

Keep moving and occupied. It makes you more efficient, focused, and sanitary in your execution. And you will have less to clean up after cooking.

68. Do not cross–contaminate.

Basic but often forgotten: wash the cutting board on which you sliced the raw chicken *before* you chop produce on it. Better: adopt the kosher standard of using separate, color–coded cutting boards for different foods (green for vegetables, red for meat, and so on).

69. Use a garbage bowl.

Do as the pros do. For convenience, sanitation, and speed when peeling vegetables, cutting fruit, or trimming meat, place the unwanted scraps in a designated bowl on your countertop or cutting board.

70. Organization breeds imagination.

Creativity is spawned in the preparation. Chopping, dicing, wiping... they are all half–conscious manual tasks that occupy the body productively without taxing the mind, which is free to roam and flit. When the small tasks have been attended to, heightened awareness reigns.

VI

Building Blocks

71. **Taste as you go.**

    Start tasting with your *mise en place* and don't stop until you serve the food. Your end product will taste of its components.

72. **Know the flavors.**

    There is no master score for manipulating flavors but you must know the notes: sweet, salty, sour, bitter. Think of the sweetness not only of honey or sugar, but of corn or port; the saltiness of Parmesan and capers as well as seaweed or anchovies; the sourness not just of lemons and vinegar, but of buttermilk and tamarind; and the bitterness found in chocolate or coffee as well as radishes and rhubarb.

    Your job as the cook is to consider these notes and compose a balance of harmony, melody, rhythm, and counterpoint. Balancing flavors is like writing a glorious song — it makes the dish, and the mind of the diner, dance.

73. Don't forget umami.

Umami means yummy. It's a savory, earthy flavor that is neither sweet, bitter, sour, nor salty, but a taste all its own. Dr. Kikunae Ikeda identified this elusive fifth flavor in 1907 while the Japanese were enjoying it in *dashi* (stock). In France around the same time, Georges Auguste Escoffier was first exploring it in his elixir, veal stock.

Umami foods contain glutamate, a non–essential amino acid. Add saltiness (sodium) to *umami* and you intensify flavor even further, as with the amplifying effect of monosodium glutamate (MSG). Serious cooks achieve *umami* by more authentic means; they derive it from pure ingredients like Celtic salt on a mushroom or freshly laid egg, and not from a bottle of MSG made from hydrolyzed wheat gluten.

Prawns, beef, fungi, and fermented cheese like Roquefort are all intensely *umami*. Simply put, delicious.

74. Know your water.

Your most frequent ingredient is your water. Its taste is defined mostly by what is known as its *terroir* [ter–WAHR], or sense of place. That is, water tends to taste of the ground, or pipes, from which it comes. Florida water, for example, often tastes of swamp. Colorado water hints at mountain runoff. All are different.

34

Water's sulfuric compounds, mineral overabundance, or chlorine might taint the flavor of the food you cook in it. Tea sommelier James Labe points out that water's mineral content, for example, can accentuate or soften the natural bitterness of greens.

Your water's influence on flavor, however, typically is insignificant compared to the vastly stronger flavors of food. Your task is to be aware of how *your* water contributes to your final result. When impurities are prominent in your water or are overwhelming to your cooking, filter your tap water.

75. Recognize that all food has texture.

Baby food and puréed carrots have texture, no less than granola or fresh apple. Texture is always there. The only question is its quality: smooth, crunchy, lumpy, firm, creamy. Note, too, that texture has two components: the visual and the tactile. The skin—like surface variation of banana flesh is distinct from its overwhelmingly smooth mouth feel.

Learn to recognize the range of textures and their components, then begin to shape and balance. When making sauce, do you strain it for refinement and subtlety, or leave it as it is to convey rusticity and authenticity? Either is valid. What experience do you wish to create?

76. Know the ratios.

Long grain rice: one part rice to two parts water (in small quantities). Dried couscous to water: one—to—one. Vinaigrette: three parts oil to one part vinegar, in general. *Mirepoix* [mihr—PWAH] is not equal parts carrot, celery, and onion (it is 25 percent, 25 percent, 50 percent); if it were, the sweetness of the carrot would overwhelm and the celery would inappropriately reveal itself in the dish. (See 139. Prepare *mirepoix*.)

Personal preference may lead to tweaking, but if you depart significantly from these fundamental proportions, you will get undesirable outcomes.

77. Think regionally.

Fields of lavender allow the southern French bee to flavor the most exquisite *provençale* honeys, which in turn are the quintessential accompaniments to any of the dozens of fresh artisanal goat cheeses from the region, which are nicely balanced by the local wines. When building a dish, plate, or menu, consider its regional integrity. Even the most adept cooks cannot improve upon nature. (Recall 21. Above all, do no harm.)

78. Think compositionally.

Caprese salad, with its sliced tomatoes and mozzarella of

similarly sized circles and flecked, pear–shaped basil leaves, excites the eye long before it delights the taste buds. Its alternating red, white, and green arrangement reminds us not only of nature, but of the colors of the region and country from which the eponymous salad hails. The contrast and repetition of shapes, colors, textures, and sizes provide a powerful form of culinary communication.

79. Think structurally.

Structure is a part of the aesthetic and functional dialogue between cook and diner, revealing of the process of creation as well as consumption.

Consider sushi. Single slices of raw fish atop individual blocks of rice, known as *nigiri*, distinguish themselves from *chirashi*, where several portions of raw fish are placed together on a large bed of rice. Then there is *maki*, where the fish and rice are rolled inside a seaweed wrapper to be sliced into bite–sized rounds, exposing the contents in cross–section. All three contain the same ingredients. But how these ingredients are structured determines the ratio of fish to rice, the texture and flavor of each bite, even the manner in which they should be tasted and eaten.

80. Think in steps.

Sophisticated cooking is often a multistep process.

Preparing steak? Sear it first stove–top to seal in flavor and moisture, then transfer it to the oven to finish. Making string beans almandine? First blanch the beans for color and flavor, then finish them in the sauté pan with the toasted nuts and butter. Each layer, each step, serves its purpose; skip one and its benefit is lost.

81. **Ask basic questions.**
Run a continual, silent self–survey as you cook: Do I have my *mise en place* in place? Has the meat been trimmed of excess fat? Have I seasoned the fish properly? Is that pan hot enough to add the oil? Have I rested the roast long enough to be carved? Is the asparagus tender? Is the flavor of the sauce clean and vibrant? Is it the proper consistency?

Continually asking questions helps you build quality at each step and keeps you in the mental game of cooking until the moment the food is eaten.

82. **First aroma and appearance, then temperature, then texture, then flavor.**
There is a fixed sequence to the sensory experience of consuming food. First is the atmospheric and aesthetic impact of how the food smells and looks.

Next, before the tongue is able to identify texture or flavor, it *feels* the temperature. When scent, appearance, or temperature is wrong, first impressions cannot be remade. Food must smell right, look good, and be at the proper temperature at the moment it is tabled and eaten. When it is, your diner will relax into a more receptive mood, the better to absorb all the other gifts of your efforts.

Next comes texture. One detects temperature at the moment food hits the lips or tongue, but determines texture when the tongue engages the food relative to the palate, teeth, and cheeks. Tactile exploration informs and influences the perception of flavor and, along with aroma, appearance, and temperature, establishes the context for how the food will taste. Warm, soggy corn flakes or crunchy (undercooked) pasta can never taste right.

Anticipation is half the journey. Taste is the destination, but there are multiple preceding stops along the way. Manage this journey. It is your job to imbue it with meaning and sensibility.

83. **Feel the sounds. Taste the smells. Touch the flavors.**

Cross—wire your sensory experience. To taste, breathe; smell the taste, taste the smell. Absorb the product and understand it deeply through multiple senses. The eyes, nose, ears, and hands are as much participants as the tongue and the teeth.

When corn, for instance, is ripe and plump, the sensory experience begins before you even take the first bite. Rip the husk off the corn in one aggressive tug. Feel the slight resistance. Hear the squeak that tells you the inside is shiny and firm and new and ready to burst. Every interaction with fresh summer corn hints at and enhances your first pleasurable bites, those sequential micro—explosions. Savor the crisp rupture of each kernel's skin and the pop of its juice in your mouth. Sense the immediate sweetness. Feel the starchy milk run down the inside of your cheeks.

"Sex is good," says Garrison Keillor, "but not as good as fresh, sweet corn."

VII

Temperature

84. Command the heat.

"The chef's job," writes Daniel Boulud, "[is] to employ heat to transform ingredients... Whether it is extracting and re-absorbing juice in roasting, or braising and reducing, or sautéing then caramelizing—you are working the moisture in the food you are preparing; and then concentrating it, reintegrating it back into the ingredient. Heat, concentrate, reintegrate. No matter how you apply heat, this is the transformational aspect of cuisine. How good your food is depends on how well you control this force of nature."

85. Move the moisture.

Food has moisture content. Cooking involves temperature changes. Temperature changes *move moisture*. Concentration (as in sautéing, grilling, broiling, roasting, or baking) is the process of sealing moisture into the food. Extraction (poaching) is the process of drawing moisture out of it. The mixed method (braising) applies both processes.

86. **Never jump food more than one temperature state at a time.**

There are four functional temperature states: 1) frozen, 2) cold, 3) room temperature, and 4) warm or hot.

When you move food from one state to another (in either direction), don't skip over a temperature state by, for instance, taking a roast directly from the refrigerator to the oven, or from the oven to the refrigerator. Only one state change at a time.

Jumping a state disrupts or destroys the vital process of moisture concentration and reintegration within the ingredient as its temperature changes. Place a sealed, warm lasagna in a cold fridge, and where does all that heat and moisture go? It collects on the top of your lovely lasagna, now no longer so lovely.

87. **Season as you go.**

As your food progresses through its temperature changes during the cooking process, seasonings (and moisture) are constantly being absorbed and redistributed. Season when you start. Season as you go. Season again when you finish. (For more on seasoning, see the Pantry chapter and 203. Correct the seasoning.)

Temperature

88. Always preheat the oven.

Wait at least fifteen minutes. Better, use a thermometer to verify that the oven has reached the target temperature. If you do not follow this rule, your food will take longer to cook and might suffer dryness or toughness or both.

89. Keep the door shut.

Do not unpack your groceries with the refrigerator door ajar. Cold air escapes as the warm kitchen air enters, the machinery has to work harder to maintain its temperature, and you compromise the safety of your refrigerated foods.

Similarly, do not baste a turkey while it is *in* the oven. Hot air escapes with every second the oven door is left open. Remove the bird first, close the oven door, set the bird on the counter to baste it, then return it to the oven. The consequences of leaving the door open can be more drastic than you think: longer cooking time, dried—out proteins, uneven results.

90. Do not crowd the pan.

If you intend to sear, keep ample space between product. If pieces of meat or fish are too close together in the pan, they produce too much moisture to caramelize. Work in batches, if necessary, to maintain proper spacing.

Also, pat dry your food before applying dry heat; excess moisture will steam what you are otherwise attempting to cook by another method.

91. **Move the pan off the heat.**
When a recipe says to remove the pan from the heat, do not just turn off the heat. Gas or electric, the heat source below the pan is still hot. Place the pot elsewhere so room—temperature air circulates around it, otherwise you risk overcooking.

Be aware that thermal mass, a kind of temperature momentum, is often at work, continuing the currently prevailing heat state unless you counter it. Cooking will continue until the energy of the heat is *negated*, not just when you remove the food from the heat source. (See 136. Always shock vegetables after they have been blanched.)

92. **Flag hot things.**
Place an oven mitt, potholder, or towel over the handle of any hot item you set aside. Signal clearly to others and yourself that there is danger in touching it.

93. **Don't grab a hot pan with a wet cloth.**
Water conducts heat; you'll scald yourself.

94. Use a cold pan for butter.

Heat the pan and butter simultaneously. Butter added to a hot pan burns on contact due to its dairy content. The proteins and sugars turn from brown to black and taste bitter instead of sweet. Burnt butter is toxic; throw it out and start again.

95. Use a hot pan for oil.

Add oil directly to an already hot pan; in a matter of seconds, it becomes hot enough to cook your food, but not yet hot enough to smoke. When it does smoke, it is toxic; throw it out and start again. (See 107. Match the oil with the cooking method.)

96. Do not add cold ingredients to hot foods, or vice versa.

If you add cold milk to a warm *roux* [ROO] (equal parts flour and butter cooked in a saucepan), you get a lumpy *béchamel* [bay–shah–MEHL] sauce. If you ladle cold stock into warm risotto, the delicate grains of rice cook unevenly. If you mix hot liquids with a cold raw–egg mixture, as in making custard, the egg cooks in the heat of those added liquids and scrambles into tiny pieces.

A notable exception to this rule is "mounting" a sauce, that is, adding cold butter to a warm sauce to finish it. The cold butter emulsifies the warm sauce and gives it sheen, a smooth texture, a thickened feel, and a rounded taste.

97. Maintain heat at a low temperature.

Lower the oven temperature to 250°F (121°C) to keep a just–cooked casserole warm without overcooking.

98. Reheat at a high temperature.

"Flash" prepared foods at 425–475°F (218–246°C) for a few minutes to get them hot quickly without cooking them further.

99. Fire trumps radiation.

The microwave can be fine for reheating certain foods; otherwise it distances you from cooking and its elemental pleasures. Don't let a machine do your job. *You* are the cook; it is *your* fire, *your* blade, *your* hands, your *finesse* that provide the meal's soul. (Recall 10. Your soul is in the food.)

VIII

Pantry

100. Don't fear salt.

Salt is the essential ingredient that James Beard called the "sovereign of seasonings." By itself, salt is overwhelming. But when added sensibly to almost anything else, it recedes into the background to let the salted ingredient's flavor shine. If you taste the salt, you've added too much. Many cooks use too little salt; the result is food that is too bland or too bitter.

101. Use kosher or sea salt.

Kosher salt lacks the anti–caking additives and whitening agents of common table salt and has a beguiling, coarse texture that allows you to *feel how it will flavor*, a quality that is easy to experience. Rub it between your fingers and you'll know.

Sea salt has more potassium, magnesium, zinc, and other nutrients than table salt. The varieties of sea salt are colored and flavored by the waters from which they are harvested, giving you multiple options to explore.

102. **Season with your fingers and eyes.**

Feel how much seasoning you are adding to a dish and watch it land on the food. This gives you tactile and visual information about where and how to mix it.

103. **Experiment with finishing salts.**

Just before you serve your food, your final seasoning provides one last chance to balance flavor and enhance texture. Some fine finishing salts worth investigating: Celtic (particularly the delicate *fleur de sel de Guérande*), Maldon, Murray River, Hawaiian red, truffle—infused, and smoked alderwood. (See 87. Season as you go.)

104. **Use a pepper mill.**

Pepper assigns to food an earthy, savory tone. As tempting as it might be to use pre—cracked pepper, don't. Freshly cracked pepper lives up to its promise: stronger in both aroma and flavor. A quick sniff of the pre—ground kind in comparison with one turn of the mill will demonstrate the qualitative difference. Consider both coarse and fine texture options: use a coarse grind on beef, a fine grind on salad.

Also experiment with green, white, and red peppercorns, which vary in flavor and intensity.

105. When the cook has done his job, there should be no need for salt or pepper on the table.

Well, theoretically.

106. Select oils with taste in mind.

Olive oils offer the verdant and earthy taste of... olive. Toasted nut oils and pressed fruit oils with more forward flavors should be reserved to finish cooked foods. Canola, vegetable, grapeseed, and peanut oils all have little to no flavor other than that of fat itself.

107. Match the oil with the cooking method.

Here's the general rule: the lighter the oil, the higher the temperature at which it begins to break down and smoke. Deep–frying occurs at a high temperature and requires an oil with a high smoke point, like peanut or vegetable oil. Olive oil, with its lower smoke point, is seldom used for deep–frying foods, but often for sautéing. (Recall 95. Use a hot pan for oil.)

108. **Use Dijon mustard.**

     It is the cook's standard, used in everything from mayon-
     naise and vinaigrette to meat rubbings and pan sauces. It
     emulsifies and flavors potently without overpowering.

109. **Cook with sugar.**

     A pinch of granulated sugar, like a pinch of salt, can balance
     flavor and brighten food. Bland tomato sauce? Sprinkle in a
     touch of sugar to amplify the tomatoes' natural sweetness.
     Sautéed onions need more flavor? Add a light dusting of
     sugar to enhance the caramelization process.

110. **Never lift a lid when cooking rice.**

     If you lift the lid before the rice has finished absorbing the
     liquid, you compromise the air pockets that have been
     steadily developing during cooking. The rice will stick to
     itself and become dense and chewy.

     To quash the urge to peek, use a glass lid. You can mon-
     itor for a stable simmer and later confirm that the rice has
     absorbed all its liquid.

111. **Always let rice rest.**

     Take the pot off the heat before removing the lid and fluff-
     ing the grains. This allows any residual moisture to release
     itself from the air pockets in the rice. If you were to fluff the

rice without letting it rest, it would be too moist and sticky. Rice grains should not stick together, unless you're making sticky rice, or sushi rice. (Recall 91. Move the pan off the heat.)

112. **Season the pasta water, not just the sauce.**
Add a tablespoon of salt to five quarts of water. Do the same for boiling potatoes, too. (Recall 71. Taste as you go.)

113. **Match the pasta's shape to the sauce's weight.**
Never heard of spaghetti alfredo? That's because creamy sauces adhere best to flat noodles, like fettucine. Long, narrow noodles like spaghetti and capellini are best with thinner sauces like pesto, oil and garlic, or carbonara. Short, shaped pastas like rigatoni, penne, and fusili pair well texturally with chunky vegetable and meat sauces.

IX

Stocks & Sauces

114. Stock is its own ingredient.

"Stocks," Escoffier writes, "are to cooking what the foundation is to a house." They are the liquid concentrations of meaty bones and aromatics such as *mirepoix* and *bouquet garni* [boh–KAY gahr–NEE] (literally, "garnished bouquet," a bundle of thyme sprigs, parsley stems, black peppercorns, and sometimes garlic cloves).

Your goal when making stock (veal stock, chicken stock, beef stock, vegetable stock, fish *fumet* [foo–MAY]) is to ensure it tastes of more than just its component parts. Prepared properly, stock achieves its own flavor beyond its individual elements and serves as a unique ingredient when added to something else.

Store–bought stock can do in a pinch, but serious cooks make their own to ensure quality and depth of flavor. For good stock and sauce recipes, look to *Sauces: Classical and Contemporary Saucemaking* by James Peterson.

115. **Keep the solids wet with hot water.**

Begin stock by filling the pot with enough *cold* water to cover the solids up to two inches. As the water evaporates during cooking and the solids become uncovered, add more *hot* water to the pot. (Recall 96. Do not add cold ingredients to hot foods, or vice versa.)

116. **Size the cuts to the cooking time.**

Cut the bones and vegetables for white chicken stock, for instance, relative to the brief cooking time of two hours. Use large bones and big chunks of vegetables for a beef or veal stock that takes eight or more hours to cook.

117. **Overcooked stock tastes bitter; undercooked stock is weak and watery.**

You can dilute an overcooked stock or fortify an undercooked one, but anything you do to repair a damaged stock won't be as good as getting it right in the first place.

118. **Never season stock.**

Stock is a base for sauces and other dishes that themselves will be seasoned. Seasoning a stock directly risks concentrating the salt and cracked pepper and therefore masking the stock's foundational flavors.

119. Always be skimming.

Achieve clarity by skimming the impurities as they rise to the top. This also gives the cleanest and brightest flavor.

120. Simmer stock.

If you boil it, the impurities that should rise to the top work their way back down into the stock.

121. Strain stock hard.

Take no prisoners. Leave nothing behind but juiceless meat, bones, and aromatics. Force every drop of moisture through the cheesecloth–lined strainer or *chinois* [sheen–WAH]; it all belongs to the stock and has no business being anywhere else. Push down on the solids — *hard*. Some of the most flavorful and valuable elements of the stock stay in the solids unless you, the committed and unrelenting cook, push them out. Let "bone dry" be your standard.

122. Reduce stock as a first step to making a pan sauce.

A stock lacks the concentration of a sauce. That means it doesn't have the right body, or intensity of flavor and viscosity, to stand on its own. Reduce the water content to concentrate the stock's flavor and bring it closer to a sauce.

123. **Deglaze the pan.**

Those crusty bits that stick to the pan when you sauté, sear, or roast are the food's gift to the cook. Called *sucs* [SOOKS], these drippings and food particles contain a sublime depth of flavor that only the processes of caramelization and fat rendering can impart.

To deglaze: Add stock, vinegar, or wine to the pan over moderate heat. Scrape and stir with a wooden spoon. Watch the liquid darken as the pan becomes clean (deglazed) from this happy marriage of ingredients. Allow the pan sauce to reduce for further concentration and thickness. Now season for added flavor, and perhaps add a touch of butter.

124. **Aim for proper thickness of sauce.**

Following reduction, sauces often are still too thin. Further reduction might leave you with too little sauce, or an over-concentrated sauce. Solution: Thicken sauce by using a *liaison*, that is, adding *beurre manié* [burr mahn—YAY] (equal parts kneaded flour and butter), a slurry (cornstarch, potato starch, arrowroot, or rice flour dissolved in liquid), heavy cream (reduced by half), or a *roux* (equal parts cooked flour and butter). Or use a beaten egg yolk.

Your test for the right thickness: the sauce coats the back of a spoon and holds its shape when you run your (very clean) finger through it.

125. A marinade is NOT a sauce.

Do not serve a marinade with cooked foods after it has touched raw foods. Once it has done its job, throw it out.

126. Use sauce with restraint.

Sauce is liquid seasoning; it should complement its food, never outshine it. Leave the diner wanting more.

X

Produce

127. Don't judge produce by appearance alone.

Procure with more than your eyes. Use your ears (listen for a squeak of freshness when pressing an artichoke's leaves together). Use your nose (smell the sweetness of a ripe cantaloupe). Use your hands (feel for soft spots to test a banana or apple for bruising or rotting).

128. Always wash your produce.

Clean fruits and vegetables by running them under cold water to eliminate undesirables like sand, dirt, and pesticides. If sanitation is not a convincing reason, consider the texturally unappetizing prospect of grit in your teeth.

One noteworthy exception: Raspberries crush easily and when wet become prone to early spoilage. Wash them gently and drain them on paper towels just prior to serving.

129. **Cut produce when you need it.**

Some fruits and vegetables oxidize rapidly when exposed to air, particularly tree fruits. Use apples and pears immediately after breaking their skin, otherwise rub them with lemon juice. Avocados oxidize quickly, too, so cover the exposed flesh (including guacamole) with plastic wrap touching the top to impede air contact. To prevent oxidation and discoloration of peeled potatoes, store them in cold water in the refrigerator.

130. **Store produce as your grocer does.**

Broccoli is typically refrigerated in your grocer's case; potatoes, onions, and tomatoes are not. Whole tomatoes, grown in the sun and ripened on the vine, lose their flavor and texture in the chill of an icebox. Refrigerate only *after* they have been sliced and therefore left unprotected by their natural seal.

131. **Store fresh, washed herbs in a damp paper towel.**

Roll loose, leafy herbs like parsley and cilantro tightly and then store in the refrigerator to keep them bright and crisp for days.

132. **Ripen fruit.**

"Ripening," writes Jeffrey Steingarten, "is a tightly structured, programmed series of changes that a fruit undergoes as it prepares to seduce every gastronomically aware animal in the neighborhood."

To speed ripening, place nearly ripe fruit in a loosely closed paper bag with a ripe apple, pear, peach, or banana and leave it overnight. These fruits emit a gas called ethylene that stimulates the ripening response and turns the less ripe fruit sweeter, juicier, more colorful, and less acidic.

133. Roll citrus fruits back and forth to loosen juices.
Before cutting a lemon, lime, or orange, roll it against a hard surface with the palm of your hand to loosen the nectar before cutting. Incidentally, the heaviest fruit at a given size is the juiciest.

134. Revive tired leafy greens in an ice bath.
Nothing can renew weary lettuce like a cold shock to the system. In the spirit of respecting food, enjoying life, and avoiding waste, it is worth a try.

135. Use heavily salted water when blanching vegetables.
Blanch vegetables in rapidly boiling water flavored like the sea to brighten their taste, unmask their full flavor, and enhance their color.

136. **Always shock vegetables after they have been blanched.**
Remove vegetables from blanching water either with a slotted spoon or strainer, or drain them in a colander. Immediately plunge them into an ice—water bath or run them under a steady stream of cold water until they are cool. Shocking your vegetables stops the cooking process and sets the color.

137. **Add fresh woody herbs at the beginning.**
Rosemary and thyme infuse a dish through heat.

138. **Add fresh leafy herbs at the end.**
Chervil and chives are brightest when raw.

139. **Prepare mirepoix.**
Mirepoix comprises 25 percent carrots, 25 percent celery, and 50 percent onions, all roughly chopped. This is fine cooking's magnificent trinity without which a certain depth of flavor would not exist. *Mirepoix* is one of the many reasons, in addition to fat and salt, that fine restaurant food tastes good; these vegetable aromatics enhance flavor with a purposefully unidentifiable savory note. Add *mirepoix* to the bottom of the pan when roasting pork loin to enrich the roast's flavor, or throw some into a store—bought chicken stock to fortify it. (Recall 114. Stock is its own ingredient.)

Mirepoix is cooked but never eaten; ideally it gives all it has to the cooking process.

140. Keep the moisture in your dice.

When preparing shallots, chopping onions, or making *mirepoix*, don't mash, *cut*. Maintain the fibrous structure of the pieces so that their moisture, which carries the essence of the ingredient's flavor, gets added to the food, not left on the cutting board.

141. Master cutting techniques.

Whether you are dicing an onion, chopping celery, turning a carrot, or sectioning an orange, your evenly and well-cut produce signals a conscientious and skilled cook at work. It lends pleasing symmetry to your food, and facilitates even cooking. Consult *Mastering Knife Skills* by Norman Weinstein. And practice.

142. Dress salad lightly.

Whether creamy and thick, or juicy and thin, salad dressing should be used sparingly — just enough to coat lightly each component of the salad. Think of dressing as wet seasoning for your greens. Every item should be evenly and lightly coated. (Recall 126. Use sauce with restraint.)

XI

Seafood

143. Know your fish types.

Whether your fish is fresh water or salt water in origin, oily or lean in texture, or round or flat in structure, if a cooking method works well for one of its type, then it will likely work well for another. If you want turbot but can only find flounder, don't fret.

144. Fish should not smell.

Well, maybe a little. More precisely, fresh fish should never be *malodorous*. A fish should smell of its source: a salty ocean, a clean river or lake.

145. Buy fish whole.

If you buy filets, you lose the key indicators of freshness: shiny scales, bulbous (not sunken) eyes, firm flesh resistant to the touch, and — *ahem* — a tight anus.

146. **Serve fish flesh side up.**

Unless you have mastered crisping salmon or red snapper skin to an even–colored, crunchy crackling, plate fish filet with the flesh side up, skin side down.

147. **Cook lobsters live.**

The standard methods are to steam, boil, broil, or grill. Steaming produces the most tender meat, but for real hedonism, do as Chef Thomas Keller does: First pour boiling water over the live lobster and let it steep for a minute or two. Then remove the partially cooked meat from the shell and poach it in butter.

148. **Cook scallops until rare.**

It is a culinary crime to overcook a scallop. A sea scallop might take no more than one minute per side in a hot pan to be prepared adequately for safety and superior flavor.

149. **Devein shrimp.**

For cosmetic and textural reasons primarily. Discard the vein by scoring the shrimp with the tip of a sharp paring knife and then scraping or pulling it.

XII

Poultry

150. Chicken is the test of a cook's versatility.

Every major cuisine boasts chicken as a staple protein. It is up to you to experiment: whole or in pieces, on the bone or boneless, with or without skin, poached or braised, grilled or broiled, roasted or sautéed, marinated or with sauce.

Virtually any seasoning or technique can be applied to what Jacques Pépin calls "the perfect canvas for a chef."

151. Color and size matter.

Healthy chickens have pink flesh and white skin with an average weight of 4 pounds. Artificially enhanced chickens tend toward yellow flesh or skin and might weigh 6 or 7 pounds, or more.

152. Always season the cavity of a bird.

Rub the exterior and interior with salt and pepper, and, if you like, herbs. The bird absorbs heat from within as well as from the outside; seasoning the inside allows the flavors to permeate the entire bird as heat pulls moisture through the food. (Recall 85. Move the moisture.)

153. Season first, then truss.

No one can claim culinary competence without knowing how to roast a chicken properly, and an essential step to roasting a bird properly is to truss it — that is, tie it. This allows a chicken to hold its shape and moisture, and roast evenly. A moist, tender, and plump bird will result. An untrussed chicken looks languid and defeated. The look of a trussed bird is one of pride and pomp.

Look to *The Fundamental Techniques of Classic Cuisine* by The French Culinary Institute for a visual tutorial on trussing.

154. Do not stuff a turkey.

Due to the bird's large size, the internal stuffing, so often made with raw meats and eggs, might not cook completely. The stuffing absorbs moisture from the raw bird and stays wet since very little of it is exposed to the heat directly. Even as the raw stuffing remains undercooked, it inhibits the circulation of air and heat within the cavity of the bird and so prolongs the required cooking time. This prolongation potentially dries out the breast.

The safe alternative: prepare *dressing*, not stuffing, by baking the supplementals separately in a casserole pan, not in the bird.

155. Let whole birds rest before carving.
The heat will remain in the bird while the juices redistribute themselves. Let it happen.

156. The best part of the chicken is the oysters.
The so—called "oysters" are the taut and tender ovoids of flesh on the back of a chicken near each thigh. Each oyster resides in its own smooth, rounded pocket of bone. Succulent and flavorful, their French name is *le sot l'y laisse* [luh SOH lee LESS]. Translation: "Only an idiot would leave it there."

157. For game birds, cook breasts and thighs separately.
Goose and pheasant have tender breasts and tough legs. Roasting them separately allows you to cook to their character. Duck breast is often cooked *à la minute* (at the moment it is to be eaten) in a sauté pan to a medium rare temperature, while the leg is braised or made into a *confit* [kawn—FEE] (cooked slowly, submerged in its own rendered fat).

158. Cook duck twice.

Duck has a bad reputation because it is fatty. But the cook can remedy that by applying more than one cooking method. Making duck *confit*? First poach the legs in the duck's own rendered (melted or liquefied) fat, then sauté them for service. Roasting a whole bird? Prick the skin with a fork and boil or steam it, then put it in a hot oven. Use two techniques instead of one to let the fat release first, and *then* crisp the skin. (Recall 80. Think in steps.)

XIII

———❧———

Meat

159. Know the parts.

Recognize the cow's primal cuts: chuck, rib, short loin, sirloin, tenderloin, round, bottom sirloin, shank, flank, plate, and brisket. Neck, shoulder, and leg meat is walking muscle and therefore tougher. Back meat, far from the hoof and the horns, is more tender. The same approach applies to other animals as well.

160. Know the grades of meat.

Prime beef has the best marbling (intramuscular fat) and is generally reserved for restaurants. *Choice* beef is the highest quality meat available in most grocery stores. *Select* is acceptable, but not nearly as juicy and tender.

Lamb uses the same grades but the criteria and scale differ because lamb fat is external to the muscle, not integrated with it. (See 162. Trim lamb of its fat.)

Pork is not graded this way in the United States since it

is generally bred to be very lean, so such designations do not apply.

161. **Leaner does not mean better.**

Some fat is good, cooking—wise. Ground beef that is more than 90 percent lean will likely be dry when cooked, especially if you like your burger cooked more than medium temperature; 80—85 percent lean is ideal. Filet mignon is tender, but it has little flavor compared to its fattier counterparts and so is properly served with a sauce.

Marbling adds juiciness and tenderness because the fat melts as the muscle heats. Marbled meat, such as rib eye or sirloin, needs only basic seasoning for maximum flavor.

162. **Trim lamb of its fat.**

Unlike beef, lamb meat has no marbling. Its white, wax—like fat is on the *outside* of its dense flesh. Only a small layer of lamb fat should be left on the meat to help flavor and baste the meat, as it is more watery than other animal fats and strong in flavor.

163. **Never freeze meat more than once.**

Freezing raw or cooked meat a second time damages the proteins, breaks down the muscle, and adversely affects flavor and texture. Many meats procured from the grocery store have been previously frozen, in which case this note takes on added urgency. Ask your butcher or grocer.

164. **Bring meat to room temperature before cooking it.**
Meat that is cold when it goes to the oven, skillet, or grill might cook unevenly. The interior will not have a chance to warm up before the outside is done. Remove roasts from the refrigerator one to two hours ahead of cooking time. A steak, on the other hand, needs just twenty minutes outside the fridge to lose its chill. (Recall 86. Never jump food more than one temperature state at a time.)

165. **Apply the proper cooking method to the cut.**
Flank, skirt, and sirloin steaks are for grilling and searing. Thick bone—in steaks like rib eye, T—bone, and porterhouse can handle broiling. Juicy, tender cuts like whole tender-loin, top loin, or rib roast should be, well, roasted. For tougher cuts like chuck and brisket, braising tenderizes the meat and reintegrates moisture. (Recall 85. Move the moisture.)

166. **Presentation side down first.**
Always cook meat first on the side you will present in service. The pan or grill is cleanest when the food first hits its surface. This also gives you an insurance policy against

overcooking the food. If the presentation side were cooked second, you might be tempted to cook the meat longer than otherwise desirable just for aesthetic reasons, which might compromise the texture and moisture of the meat.

167. **Turn meat once.**

If you turn it over and over, meat will toughen. (Bacon is an exception; when cooked in a pan, turn it frequently to render the fat.) There is a good tactile cue to indicate when to turn the food: if it's sticking, it's not ready. Wait until the meat has seared and released itself from the cooking surface (similar to waiting until a pancake has bubbled and therefore browned). Lift it gently out of respect for the food and your desire to prepare a quality product.

168. **Well done is an oxymoron.**

Cooking steaks and chops to a well–done temperature (170°F or 76°C) nullifies some of the best qualities we revere in meat: juicy flesh, tender texture, and depth of flavor. Above 135°F or 57°C is sufficient and safe for meat.

169. **Do not overcook pork.**

Overcooking to the point of grayish flesh produces dry and tough meat, even for juicy center cuts like loin and chops. A medium pork chop cooked to 145°F (about 63°C) has a faintly pink center and poses no safety hazard. Just use a thermometer.

170. Cook bacon in a cold pan.

If you put cold bacon in a hot pan, its exterior might burn and blacken quickly, sealing in the fat you wish to release. Start with a cold pan to allow the bacon to come to temperature *with* the pan so that it renders its fat before browning.

Cooking bacon in a skillet, by the way, yields curly bacon; cooking it in an oven leaves the strips flat.

171. Let meat rest before carving.

After any meat is cooked, allow it to rest for at least ten minutes so the internal juices redistribute evenly before carving. If carved immediately from the oven, all the concentrated juices run from the meat, making what could have been very juicy meat dry and tough.

XIV

Bread & Pastry

172. Mise en place your baking ingredients.

It is especially easy to miss something when your dry goods are all white powders.

173. Measure with precision.

When baking, always measure the ingredients exactly as the recipe dictates. Success in baking is chemical; this is not the place to get creative. Best practice: use a scale if the recipe offers weight measurements.

174. Ensure baking ingredients are at room temperature.

Unless otherwise directed. Again, chemistry affects everything. Eggs, especially, need to be room temperature when you bake, and definitely if you want to whip whites, although they are easier to separate when cold. So separate them cold, but let them sit and then work with them at room temperature.

175. **Use the spoon–and–sweep method to measure.**

     Whenever you measure flour, spoon the flour into the measuring cup. This aerates the flour, making it lighter than would scooping the measuring cup directly into the vessel of flour, which compacts the flour and impacts your results. *Spoon* the flour higher than the top of the cup and then *sweep* the excess with the back of a flat implement, such as a knife, to achieve the perfect measurement.

176. **Sift as the recipe specifies.**

     Sift dry ingredients to ensure that there are no clumps that would remain in a batter. Some recipes call for flour or other dry ingredients to be measured first and then sifted ("2 cups flower, sifted"). Other recipes call for flour to be sifted first, then measured ("2 cups sifted flour"). There is a volume disparity between the two sequences; 4 ounces of sifted flour is the volumetric equivalent of 5 ounces unsifted. Follow the recipe. If it does not specify sifted or unsifted, *do not sift*, because it is a sure sign that the recipe writer did not either.

177. **Combine dry ingredients before adding anything wet.**

     Unless the recipe prescribes otherwise, mix wet ingredients together in one bowl and dry ingredients in another bowl before combining them. This ensures the even distribution of the dry ingredients in a batter.

Most batters contain a leavening agent, such as baking soda or powder. When dry leavening agents come into contact with liquid, a chemical reaction begins. If you mix dry and wet separately and combine them right before the batter goes to the oven or pan, you maximize the rising effect.

178. **Use weights when blind–baking a pie shell.**

"Blind" as in empty, no filling. Line the raw shell or quiche crust with parchment paper (or a large coffee filter). Fill it with dried beans or pie weights pushed against the sides before baking to maintain the shape and inhibit unwanted puffing. This also prevents a soggy–bottomed crust.

179. **Let bread cool.**

If you cut right away, the steam escapes and condensation might render the crust soggy. A loaf of bread that is merely being re–warmed, on the other hand, may be sliced immediately for that "fresh from the oven" effect.

180. **Never frost a cake before it has cooled completely.**

Frosting added to a hot cake melts or separates. Cool a cake on a rack after it has been removed from the pan. Let air circulate on all its sides for at least an hour, then frost it. An exception: frost a warm — not hot — cake to achieve a glaze–like effect.

XV

Dairy & Eggs

181. Appreciate the benefits of butter.

Much of the pleasure of food comes from fats like butter. Fat provides enticing mouth feel and is a vehicle of taste since many of the substances that affect our taste receptors are fat–soluble. Unlike other fats, butter provides additional proteins and dairy solids that enhance and balance flavors, smooth acids, and counter bitterness. There is no replacement for dairy fat; nothing feels quite as creamy or has the same flavor.

182. Cook with unsalted butter.

To control the seasoning of a dish, use unsalted butter when you cook. Leave salted butter for the table.

183. Judge a cheese by its rind.

The outside of a cheese tells you all you need to know about its quality, age, and texture. Cheese Monger Steven Jenkins advises, "Up with natural rinds, buffed, brushed, washed or cloth—covered. Down with plastic, paraffin (wax) and paint."

184. **Serve cheese at room temperature.**

But store it in the refrigerator. Cold storage preserves freshness, whereas room temperature releases flavor and softens texture.

185. **Consume soft cheeses immediately.**

The softer the cheese, the more quickly it perishes. Hard cheeses have longer lives and, stored in the refrigerator, last at least a few weeks.

186. **Grate cheese yourself.**

Pre—shredded cheeses offer convenience but lack flavor. Stabilizers and additives are needed to keep such cheese from clumping together. This commercial concern is not yours if you grate cheese as you use it. (Recall 17. Embrace the mundane.)

187. **Add cheese at the end.**

If you add cheese early in the cooking process, prolonged or excessive heat might "break" the cheese (separate its fat from its dairy solids) and degrade the dish. Instead, melt the cheese over low heat — or brown it under a high flame using a broiler or salamander — once the dish is substantially finished. Use freshly grated or shredded cheese for even, speedy melting.

188. **Test eggs for freshness.**

If you're uncertain, crack an egg onto a flat plate. Its contents should hold their rounded or domed shapes; but if the white spreads and the yolk flattens, the egg is suspect.

189. **Use fresh eggs for poaching.**

When an egg is fresh, the white (albumen) clings to the yolk, which aids in achieving the coveted oval shape of a poached egg.

190. **Use older (but not expired) eggs for boiling.**

With age, the air pocket between the shell and the membrane gets bigger, making the egg easier to peel. You are less likely to take some of the "white" with you when you unshell it.

191. **Use large eggs when the recipe does not specify size.**

The minimum weight for a large egg is 2 ounces, whereas the minimum weight for an extra large egg is 2.25 ounces. If you casually use extra large eggs, and the recipe calls for half a dozen large eggs, you are increasing your egg quantity by almost another whole egg.

192. Separate eggs with your hands.

Pass the egg back and forth over your immaculately clean hands, and let the white drain between your fingers into one bowl. The yolk is less likely to break this way than if passed between two cracked shells. Then place the remaining dry yolk in another bowl. Wash your hands of the raw residue before moving on.

XVI

———✦———

Wine & Spirits

193. If you won't drink it, don't cook with it.

Reject the common myth that inferior wine and spirits can be used in cooking with no ill effect. (Recall 45. A dish is only as good as what goes into it.) Contrariwise, there is no need to use Louis XIII cognac to make brandied apples. As Escoffier writes, "Profligate extravagance is as bad as a restrictive economy."

194. Connect the foundations.

Consider cooking with the same wine you will serve. Not the exact bottle necessarily, but the grape at least. Even though such attentive touches are rarely noticed, they provide a semi–conscious but satisfying coherence to the meal. (Recall 77. Think regionally.)

195. Add wine at the beginning of the cooking process.

The presence of alcohol in food makes it bitter, so give the wine time to reduce and the alcohol a chance to evaporate.

196. Don't boil wine.

When you reduce wine, simmer, don't boil, or you lose some of the virtues you want to preserve, including the inherent flavor of the grape.

197. Expect wine's alcohol, but not its character, to evaporate.

The more full–bodied a wine is in the bottle, the more full–bodied is its effect on the food with which you cook it. Character carries. Similarly, a light wine retains its sense of crispness and conveys it to the food.

198. Cool red.

Place a room–temperature bottle of red wine in the refrigerator for twenty minutes before you serve it. Despite the prevailing myth, room temperature is too warm for red wine. A range of $60-65°F$ ($16-18°C$) is about right. Avoid rapid temperature swings in any case.

199. Warm white.

Remove white wine from the refrigerator twenty minutes before you serve it; $58°F$ ($14°C$) is ideal.

200. Color outside the lines.

When cooking (or drinking), try red wine with fish, white wine with beef. The result might not please you, but break the rules anyway. Taste what happens. You already know the red wine classic *coq au vin*; your experimentation might yield the next *coq au Riesling*. (Recall 7. When you're ready, mess with the recipe.)

201. Use it in a year.

Unless you have a 1982 Château Lafite Rothschild, your wine will not get better with time. It will likely get worse. Everything has its peak.

XVII

---◆◆◆---

Repairing Food

202. Always taste the food before you serve it.

You carefully planned a menu. Studied the recipes. Hand—
selected the finest ingredients. Washed and stored them
with the utmost care. Prepared your *mise en place*. Cooked
with focus, skill, and joy — but you are not done. Before
presenting, *taste the food*. Confirm your result, or take the
needed action to improve it.

203. Correct the seasoning.

The professional use of "correct" is misleading. It does not
mean that something needs fixing in that it was ruined or
executed poorly. It means it has to be made right, not from
a state of wrong, just from a state of not right *yet*. "Adjust"
is a better word.

Expect that the seasoning you added earlier has been
absorbed into the dish. (Recall 87. Season as you go.) Taste

and then re—season with salt and pepper one last time before serving your food.

Spices are normally added *during* the cooking process, not after, to integrate their flavors into the dish. Adding them raw at the end can be bitter and unpleasant. Ensure the salt and pepper are in balance with the dish before you add more spice.

204. Nothing is a lost cause.

Unless it is burnt or salted beyond rescue, you can always bump up other flavors to balance the dish.

205. Acidic food?

Season with salt and pepper. Or tone it down with something smooth, like dairy or fat. Or add sweetness to counter the excessive acidity.

206. Dull food?

Brighten with acid or salt. Enrich with fat. Restaurants use animal fat and salt to enhance flavor. Vinegar, lemon juice, finishing oils, butter, and sugar are also old standbys.

207. Bitter food? Spicy food?

Salt inhibits bitterness. Honey counterbalances spice.

208. Salty food?

For solid food, such as finished rice, add more finished but unsalted food to de—concentrate the saltiness. For liquid food, dilute. This might weaken the other flavors and affect texture, so dilute with whatever liquid you started with — milk, juice, stock, tomato sauce — and reseason. (Recall 96. Do not add cold ingredients to hot foods, or vice versa.)

XVII

Presentation

209. True refinement is invisible.

A showy turnip and a(n overly) friendly waiter have their virtues, but refinement is not among them. Refined cooking, like refined behavior, does not call attention to itself.

210. Select the plate with purpose.

Here's the rule: the more intricate the food, the simpler the plate. When in doubt, use a plain white dish.

211. Avoid even numbers when plating food.

Bilateral symmetry can suggest animal or human forms; shun such anthropomorphizing unless you are making gingerbread men. Imbalance adds interest. One exception: eggs, sunny—side up, look good in twos for some reason (likely Freudian).

212. Hide the misery.

Concealment beats disposal of an otherwise fine piece of damaged food, particularly when the clock militates against alternatives. Did you tear a piece of skin from the chicken thigh? Garnish it with chopped herbs. Burn a corner of a salmon filet? Nap it with a little sauce.

213. Garnish with intention.

Use *functional* garnishes. The proverbial lemon wedge that accompanies a filet of fish counters brininess by adding citrus brightness. The archetypal sprig of parsley, once considered a refreshing palate cleanser between courses, has now acquired some cliché baggage that easily signals an afterthought. Better to chop the parsley and sprinkle it over the dish when it plays a role in flavoring the food. Send an invitation that it be eaten.

214. Never sabotage a dish for the sake of color.

Avoid the temptation to add "red" or "yellow" to a dish. Color, for its own sake, is your lowest priority. It has to look good, but you are making food to be eaten. Do not sacrifice a dish with, say, finely diced red pepper where it does not belong, flavor—wise.

215. No fingerprints on the plate.

Wipe it before you table it. A little white vinegar on a clean, damp, rolled cloth is how the pros do it.

216. Food never lies.

No excuse or explanation makes the slightest bit of difference. All that matters is on the plate and in the diner's mouth. Be grateful for cooking's objectivity; in its mercilessness one earns mastery and dignity.

XIX

Last Thought

217. Always be cooking.

Hone your craft by doing it. Stop reading. Start cooking.

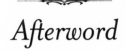

Afterword

Life can be overwhelming. Correction: Life *is* overwhelming. We are overstimulated, overeducated, overachievers wanting more. At least that is how I feel about my life from time to time. Then I dream about retreating to a cabin in the woods or, better yet, a shack on an idyllic warm isle surrounded by turquoise seas. New York and Nevis. I need both.

Without buying a plane ticket how do you balance? Aphorisms. I love them. A pithy statement can become a mantra. In fact, I have a few favorites that have helped center my life. I studied Taekwondo many years ago in Asia with a Korean master. His English was limited. His words were few but he said things that I carry to this day. My favorite was, "Eat the meat, the rest is nonsense!" Now, I don't literally agree with him, but when I find myself acting like a swirling dervish, I find the meat and cut out the nonsense.

Like many foodies, I decompress in the kitchen. My inner Zen expresses itself with cutting a carrot or smelling freshly chopped dill. The hundreds of cookbooks I own are inspirational but not centering. Then *Notes on Cooking* came along. I love the short statements that lead to long reflections. They bring me back to basics that pare away the "nonsense" in the kitchen. Truly great cooking takes thought, practice, and dedication, not gadgets or food processors. Listen to the common sense of *Notes on Cooking* and you will find yourself a happier cook.

DOROTHY HAMILTON
FOUNDER & CEO
THE FRENCH CULINARY INSTITUTE
NOVEMBER 2008

APPENDIX I

Flavor Lexicon

A scene from the film *Shopgirl*:

Two characters are in an art gallery, drinking mojitos.

One asks, "How was it?"

The other says, "Noisy."

Chew on these other delicious food adjectives:

Acerbic. Acidic. Acrid. Aged. Aromatic. Astringent. Biting. Bitter. Bland. Blunt. Brackish. Bright. Briny. Browned. Bubbly. Burnt. Buttery. Caramelized. Caustic. Charred. Cheesy. Citric. Clean. Cloying. Creamy. Crisp. Crispy. Cruciferous. Crunchy. Dark. Deep. Delectable. Dry. Doughy. Dulcet. Earthy.

Fizzy. Flaky. Fluffy. Floral. Forward. Fragile. Fresh. Fried. Frosty. Fruity. Full–bodied. Gamy. Glazed. Grassy. Greasy. Gritty. Hearty. Herbaceous. Hot. Icy. Juicy. Layered. Leathery. Lean. Light. Loud. Luscious. Mashed. Mellow. Mild. Milky. Minty. Moist. Musky. Nectarous. Nutty. Oily. Palatable. Peppery. Pickled. Piquant. Potable. Prickly. Puckery. Pulpy. Pungent. Quiet. Rancid. Rich. Ripe. Rubbery. Rustic. Saccharine. Salty. Satiny. Savory. Scrumptious. Seasoned. Sharp. Silky. Sinewy. Sizzling. Smoky. Smooth. Smothered. Soft. Sour. Spicy. Spongy. Steamy. Sticky. Stinging. Stuffed. Succulent. Sugary. Supernacular. Sweet. Syrupy. Tangy. Tantalizing. Tart. Tasteful. Tasteless. Tender. Tepid. Thin. Tough. Treacly. Toothsome. Umami. Unctuous. Velvety. Verdant. Vibrant. Warm. Waxy. Wet. Whipped. Woody. Yummy. Zesty.

Food is never really finished until you talk about it.

APPENDIX II

Classic Combinations

Consider this sublimity: fresh cherries with basil and black pepper. Sweet, but with a wine–like earthiness. The basil provides licorice or fennel tones, a suggestion of candy and biting qualities yearning for spice. The pepper edges this match upward to where the cherry wants to be savory, not sweet like a confection.

Explaining the symbiosis and synergy of powerful food combinations is one thing, but experience and experiment with as many of them as you can. Better yet, discover your own.

duck & orange
orange & fennel
fennel & arugula
arugula & balsamic vinegar
balsamic vinegar &
    strawberries
strawberries & cream

cream & garlic
garlic & haricots verts
haricots verts & almonds
almonds & trout
trout & horseradish
horseradish & roast beef
roast beef & potatoes

potatoes & duck fat
duck fat & parsnips
parsnips & beets
beets & lemon
lemon & poppy seeds
poppy seeds & radishes
radishes & sea salt
sea salt & caramel
caramel & chocolate
chocolate & red wine
red wine & filet mignon
filet mignon & truffles
truffles & leeks
leeks & chestnuts
chestnuts & venison
venison & shallots
shallots & corn
corn & chipotle
chipotle & mayonnaise
mayonnaise & french fries
french fries & mussels
mussels & saffron
saffron & lamb
lamb & cardamom
cardamom & rose water
rose water & pistachios
pistachios & artichokes
artichokes & mozzarella
mozzarella & tomatoes
tomatoes & cucumbers
cucumbers & lingonberries
lingonberries & wild goose
wild goose & wild rice

wild rice & sausage
sausage & spinach
spinach & pine nuts
pine nuts & couscous
couscous & chicken
chicken & peanut
peanut & cilantro
cilantro & avocado
avocado & grapefruit
grapefruit & jicama
jicama & mahi–mahi
mahi–mahi & mango
mango & Thai basil
Thai basil & Japanese
   eggplant
Japanese eggplant & miso
miso & shiso
shiso & yuzu
yuzu & tamari
tamari & pecans
pecans & pumpkin
pumpkin & prawns
prawns & sirloin
sirloin & blue cheese
blue cheese & Asian pears
Asian pears & pomegranate
pomegranate & yogurt
yogurt & meyer lemon
meyer lemon & green olives
green olives & manchego
manchego & quince
quince & vanilla bean
vanilla bean & peaches

Appendix II : Classic Combinations

peaches & brown sugar
brown sugar & bacon
bacon & eggs
eggs & Cotswold cheddar
Cotswold cheddar &
    walnuts
walnuts & honey
honey & apples
apples & cinnamon
cinnamon & star anise
star anise & mint
mint & Grand Marnier
Grand Marnier & crêpes
crêpes & mushrooms
mushrooms & goat cheese
goat cheese & figs
figs & foie gras
foie gras & brioche
brioche & butter
butter & marjoram
marjoram & pearl barley
pearl barley & pearl onions

pearl onions & sweet peas
sweet peas & pancetta
pancetta & capers
capers & smoked salmon
smoked salmon & bagels
bagels & cream cheese
cream cheese & caviar
caviar & oysters
oysters & turkey
turkey & Turkish apricots
Turkish apricots &
    Spanish onions
Spanish onions & brisket
brisket & bread
bread & Dijon mustard
Dijon mustard & pork
pork & juniper berries
juniper berries & pineapple
pineapple & coconut
coconut & lemongrass
lemongrass & ginger
ginger & duck

APPENDIX III

Cooking Essentials

Equipment

Chef's knife.	It does everything well but slice bread, and it can do even that in a pinch. Above all, it must be SHARP.
Cutting board.	It's your desk, your home plate. Wood or plastic only, never glass, stone, or ceramic.
Sauté pan.	10–inch, heavy bottom, stainless steel with an aluminum core.
Wooden spoon.	With a long handle to stir, mix, and scrape any size vessel.
Bowls.	To mix, and for *mise en place*.
Whisk.	Essential for vinaigrettes, meringues, and batters.
Spatula.	The flexible, heatproof kind, to lift and turn food.

Tongs.   To grab, toss, or turn food.

Microplane.   To grate hard cheeses, zest fruits, and shave salt and spices.

Colander.   To rinse or drain food.

Sheet pan.   To roast and bake most foods.

Cast iron skillet.   Well seasoned for a timeless non-stick surface.

Dutch oven.   Ideal for braising, but also good for boiling and frying.

Thermometer.   To monitor the internal temperature of meat, poultry, or bread.

Appliances

Blender.   To mix or emulsify wet things.

Food processor.   To cut, chop, grate, mix, sift, or blend wet or dry things. Mostly, to save time.

Mini coffee grinder.   Not to grind coffee, but to grind spices.

Appendix *III* : *Cooking Essentials*

Supplies

Plastic wrap.	To cover stored food and to seal out air.
Aluminum foil.	To wrap a head of garlic for roasting, cover a pot for moisture retention, line a sheet pan, or provide added protection to sealed foods in storage.
Cheesecloth.	To filter stocks, sauces, and custards.
Disposable gloves.	For sanitation and cleanup.
Parchment paper.	A good shield for a sheet pan, a makeshift lid for a saucepan, or a lining for a buttered cake pan.
Side towels.	To pick up hot things safely.
Cotton twine.	To truss poultry and meats.

Recommendations

A good cook is naturally curious, particularly regarding sensuous matters. Art, travel, history, chemistry... all are fertile ground for a cook's exploration. Don't miss the standard cookbooks, of course, including *Joy of Cooking*, *The Silver Spoon*, and Julia Child's *Mastering the Art of French Cooking*, as well as classic texts by Georges Auguste Escoffier, James Beard, Jacques Pépin, M.F.K. Fisher, Richard Olney, Harold McGee, and *Le Repertoire de La Cuisine* by Louis Saulnier.

Here are some additional recommendations:

The Fundamental Techniques of Classic Cuisine by The French Culinary Institute, Judith Choate, Glenn Wolf, and Matthew Septimus
Stewart, Tabori & Chang, 2007

An entire culinary curriculum in a book, with the collected thinking, recipes, and techniques of many of the greatest living classical practitioners.

Mastering Knife Skills: The Essential Guide to the Most Important Tools in Your Kitchen by Norman Weinstein
Stewart, Tabori & Chang, 2008
An excellent visual guide to the fundamentals.

Letters to a Young Chef by Daniel Boulud
Basic Books, 2003
Career guidance from the Master Chef. Includes lucid and luscious descriptions of (what else?) food.

Sauces: Classical and Contemporary Saucemaking, 3rd edition, by James Peterson
Wiley, 2008
An indispensable reference.

The Omnivore's Dilemma: A Natural History of Four Meals by Michael Pollan
Penguin, 2006
An almost too–vivid description of what we eat, and a thoughtful exploration of how our food choices matter.

Recommendations

Cooking for Kings: The Life of Antonin Carême, the First Celebrity Chef by Ian Kelly
Walker & Company, 2003

> Culinary time travel. A quick, fun, must—read for food history buffs. It has it all: society, politics, menus, and recipes.

The New Food Lover's Companion, 4th edition, by Sharon Tyler Herbst
Barron's, 2007

> A handy dictionary of every conceivable culinary topic and ingredient.

The Man Who Ate Everything by Jeffrey Steingarten
Vintage Books, 1998

> Entertaining and educational essays on food by one of the industry's most erudite and irreverent critics.

What Einstein Told His Cook: Kitchen Science Explained by Robert L. Wolke
W. W. Norton & Company, 2002

> Witty, practical, and fascinating Q&A on the science of food and cooking. Written by a professor of chemistry who is also a food columnist.

Don't Try This at Home: Culinary Catastrophes from the World's Greatest Chefs Edited by Kimberly Witherspoon and Andrew Friedman
Bloomsbury, 2005

> Nothing can lift the spirits of the beginner like a dose of *schadenfreude*. Think you've bungled? Probably not as badly as some of the very best.

Chef's Story: 27 Chefs Talk About What Got Them into the Kitchen by Dorothy Hamilton and Patric Kuh
HarperCollins, 2007

> The greatest living chefs tell how they got started. Note how often the spark begins with the realization, "Hey, I can do this."

Acknowledgments

We arrived at this volume on the shoulders of wise teachers, talented cooks, cherished colleagues, and loving friends who gifted us with their experience, dedication, generosity, and kindness.

For reviewing the manuscript, we thank Sixto Alonso, Ken Braun, Marcia S. Cohen, Sean Costello, Matt Kane, Jeff Martin, Daniel Schatzman, Tim Shaw, Jody Sheinbaum, Jane Slotin, Tom Strodel, and Laura Memory Walters.

For their kind endorsements, we are deeply grateful to Dan Barber, Lidia Matticchio Bastianich, Daniel Boulud, Gael Greene, Jacques Pépin, Jim Peterson, and Michael Romano. We also thank Julia Reich for the original jacket design, Eric Kittelberger and Daniel Tamman for their illustrations and designs, Matt and Lee Kane for their web work, and Brian and Nina Taylor of Pneuma Books for their interior design and editorial contributions.

Special thanks go to Penelope Pate Greene, Dorothy Hamilton, and Daniel Tamman for their extraordinary efforts in support of the book.

For their various efforts on our behalf and on behalf of the book, we gratefully acknowledge Alice Acheson, Serafina Alonso, Linda Amster, Nicole Braun, Alexandra Bruskoff, Shelly Burgess Nicotra, Yolanda Mariak Chendak, Robin Cohen, Jim Eber, Georgette Farkas, Paul Favale, Jennifer Garbowski, George Gibson, Kathy and Steven Goldstein, Irene Hamburger; Judy, Marc, Jacob and Jori Goodman; Anne Grossman, Elizabeth Knight, Leora Kulak, James Labe, Sandra Labriola, Pamela Lugo, Alexandra Maxwell, Debra Mintcheff, Julie Negrin, Michel Nischan, Maureen Bennett O'Connor, Maggie Odell, Ashley O'Neal, Jennifer Pelka, Michelle Pagan, Peter E. Raymond, Lauren Riback, Joan S. Richter, Lisa Schwartz, and Amy Tarr.

For their love, friendship and support, we thank Alisa Adler, Jason Arenstein, Paula de Azevedo, Phyllis Blackman, Ken and Hara Braun, Nicole Braun, Marcia S. Cohen, Jonathan Avery Costello, Sean Costello, Dana B. Davis, Charlotte and Bernard Feinstein, Betsy Feinstein, Scott Fichten, Limor Geller, Lara Glazier, Greg Goetchius, Timothy P. Graf, Adam Jacobs, Tamara McKenna, Carol Leibenson, Fanny Lopez, Molly Lyons, Gary and Evelyn Reich, Zibby Right, Lili Sandoval, Theodore R. Sayers, Lindsay

Acknowledgments

Smithen, Rachel Spector, Paula Vayas, Noel E. Volpe, and
Joe Witt.

I

Index

Index

Index

O

oil, 47, 53
olive oil, seasoning, 53
Olney, Richard, 2, 127
onions, 2, 36, 54, 64, 66, 67
organic farming, 19
organization, 29, 30
oven, 45, 48
overcooking, 46, 48, 82
oxidation, of produce, 64
oyster (of chicken), 75

P

pans, crowding of, 45–46
pantry, 51–55
paring, 29
parsley, 64, 106
pasta, 55
pastry and bread, 85–88
patience, 10, 27
peeling, 29
Pépin, Jacques, 73, 127
pepper, 52–53, 101–102
perishables, 22
Peterson, James, 57, 128
pie shells, 87
plating food, 105
poaching, 43–44, 93
pork, 79–80, 82–83
potato, 29, 55, 60, 64
poultry, 73–76
practice, 3, 8

preheating, of oven, 45
preparation, 8–9, 28–30, 85
presentation
    in eating, 38–40
    fish, 70
    meal planning, 36–37
    rules for, 105–107
procurement and storage,
    19–24
    fish, 69
    poultry, 73
    produce, 64–65
    produce, 63–67

R

raspberries, 63
ratios, of foods, 36
raw foods, storage, 22
recipes, 1–4, 99
reduction, stocks, 59
refrigeration, 22, 45, 66
refinement, xxii, 10, 105
reheating, 48
repairing food, 101–103
repetition, xxvii, 3, 8, 37
rice, cooking of, 36, 54–55
rice flour, 60
ripening, of fruits, 64–65
risotto, 47
roast, 13, 38, 43, 44, 60, 66,
    73–76, 81
roux, 47, 60

Index

For more notes on cooking and the latest updates, visit

notesoncooking.com

For quantity purchases or special needs, contact:
Pathway Book Service
4 White Brook Road
Gilsum, NH 03448
Toll free: 1–800–345–6665
Email: pbs@pathwaybook.com

Notes on Cooking is also available to the trade through
Baker & Taylor and Ingram.

The body of this book is set in *Spectrum*, which is based on the design by Jan van Krimpen in 1943 for the Spectrum Publishing House. Spectrum was completed and released by the Monotype Corporation in 1955, although the Bible project it was originally commissioned for was never completed. Spectrum is known for its readability; its roots reach directly to Venetian typefaces of the 15th century. Its varied–weight curves and angular serifs evoke the calligraphic pen strokes of its forebearers.

Mrs. Eaves, used on the cover and for chapter titles in the interior, was designed by Zuzana Licko for Emigré in 1996 as a reprise of the Transitional typeface *Baskerville*, crafted in 1757. The name, Mrs. Eaves, comes from John Baskerville's maid, Sarah Eaves, who became his wife after the death of her first husband. Like Spectrum, Baskerville was originally designed for use in a Bible. The beauty and versatility of Mrs. Eaves allow for its use as both a display and a body typeface.

Jacket design by Julia Reich and Daniel Tamman

Illustrations by Eric Kittelberger and Daniel Tamman

Interior design by Pneuma Books, LLC. *pneumabooks.com*

Printed in the United States by Thomson–Shore, Inc.